Phillipa Ridge's foray into the world of poetry was ignited by the collision of two of life's great enigmas: the act of falling in love and the occurrence of a life-changing event, the 2020 Coronavirus Pandemic. Despite the challenges of lockdown, she dedicated herself to creating poetry, documenting the rollercoaster ride that is finding and losing love, whilst simultaneously focusing her attention on the events of this extraordinary time, both politically and socially.

"Lockdown has forced us to rethink our lives, and to analyse what is intrinsic to our happiness, whilst staring down the barrel of a loaded gun. Poetry was my calm amidst the chaos."

Phillipa lives in Lancashire. She is currently working on her second book.

This book is dedicated to my forever man, wherever he is, and to those loved along the way.

Phillipa Ridge

LOOK INSIDE

AUSTIN MACAULEY PUBLISHERS™
LONDON • CAMBRIDGE • NEW YORK • SHARJAH

Copyright © Phillipa Ridge 2023

The right of Phillipa Ridge to be identified as author of this work has been asserted by the author in accordance with sections 77 and 78 of the Copyright, Designs and Patents Act 1988.

All rights reserved. No part of this publication may be reproduced, stored in a retrieval system, or transmitted in any form or by any means, electronic, mechanical, photocopying, recording, or otherwise, without the prior permission of the publishers.

Any person who commits any unauthorised act in relation to this publication may be liable to criminal prosecution and civil claims for damages.

A CIP catalogue record for this title is available from the British Library.

ISBN 9781398459229 (Paperback)
ISBN 9781398459236 (ePub e-book)

www.austinmacauley.com

First Published 2023
Austin Macauley Publishers Ltd®
1 Canada Square
Canary Wharf
London
E14 5AA

Thank you to all at Austin Macauley Publishers who have helped bring 'Look Inside' to fruition.

A big thank you to all those who have followed and supported me on Instagram @missparnassian

Thank you to the brilliant Charlotte Davies for the illustrations, in my eyes they are the perfect accompaniment to my poems.

An enormous thanks to my family, friends and colleagues, all of whom have been incredibly supportive in my foray into the world of poetry, I doubt I would have continued without them.

And finally, to all the world's wordsmiths in whose footsteps I graciously trod, my undying gratitude. Without authors, songwriters, poets and commentators, my words would be floating in the ether.

Table of Contents

Introduction	**11**
Section One – Life	**15**
A Pilot's Life	*18*
A Sister Is	*20*
How Many Times	*23*
Lazy Cat	*26*
Spring	*28*
Beggar Me	*31*
Ask My Dad	*34*
Park Bench	*37*
Notes on Ageing	*40*
Section Two – Love	**43**
Go Online	*45*
Chance	*47*
I Would...	*49*
Home For the Heart	*52*

Woman's Joy	*55*
All Things Sweet	*58*
You	*60*
Look Inside	*62*
How Strange Love Is	*64*
The Things You Do	*65*
If	*67*
Think Of Me	*68*
Section Three – Hope	**71**
The Wonder of Youth	*74*
Did You Ever	*76*
God Bless America	*79*
Dreaded Virus	*82*

Introduction

For as long as I can recall, words have held a fascination for me. They are magical, precious gems, available to all, in abundance, free of charge and ours to keep forever and to use as often as required. In primary school, I would look forward to the weekly spelling tests, a list of ten words to be anticipated, learned and regurgitated precisely. I collected those words avidly and coveted new ones to add to my ever-growing collection; mine to cherish forever. This love of language has merely intensified over the years and my delight upon encountering a word I have never heard or seen before, remains immense.

The language we use to communicate our wishes, desires and emotions seems almost limitless. The joy of choosing which words to use, is to me, a matter of precision, and when done well by poets, novelists, songwriters or journalists, is worthy of noticing. In the right hands, words and language come alive, speak to us, enliven and often heighten our emotions, as well as allow us to relate, to others, to stories and to our own situations. In short, words are what bring us together, they are what make us human. Whilst animals possess the ability to communicate, in often elaborate forms, to one another, they do not use words. This novelty is particular to human beings and should, in my estimation, be treasured. Without words, we would struggle to say what we need or want to. How many times have each of us heard the lyrics of a song and thought it could have been written solely for us? How many times have we read a novel which has brought us to tears? Words are incredibly powerful and should not be underestimated. In this age of modernity, it is often words which hurt us, either via social media or when arguing with a loved one. Rev J Martin, wrote, 'Words are free, it's how you use them that may cost you'. English Author, Edward Bulwer-Lytton back in 1839, also recognised the truism of words when he claimed that 'the pen is mightier than the sword', for language truly is the most effective tool we have and yet we face an unprecedented time where the use of language is changing and possibly even diminishing.

The art of letter writing is quickly being eroded, sadly replaced by text message or social media but can a heart emoji really replace a love letter? Or a 'like' accurately reflect the extent or depth of the feelings we hold? I suspect not. I believe that we will always need words, books, poems, songs and love letters and perhaps one day, we will recognise the true value of them. My advice to anyone who may be struggling, if you can't tell someone how you feel, write it down, words are your greatest friend, they will support you, comfort you and guide you, if you let them.

English continues to hold a unique position within the world. It is the lingua franca of the modern era, used when crossing shipping lanes and air space but also in fields such as business, science, technology and it remains the most widely spoken language across the world, with 1.6 billion speakers. Wherever I have been in the world, English has been recognised and understood. But aside from its unique significance on the world's stage, it is my native language, the one I know and love, and yet on a regular basis, I encounter or learn new words, which is always something of a surprise, although there is no reason why it should be. Of course, we can never be all-knowing when it comes to language. It is fluid, forever shifting and changing, always just slipping from our grasp, elusive and alluring. This is my first attempt at placing my own words on a blank page. My only hope being that in sharing them, someone somewhere may relate to them.

Section One – Life

Life is impossible to define. It is amazingly varied, mind-numbingly mundane, exciting, tragic, awe-inspiring, soul-destroying, magical, ever-changing and unremitting. Each of our lives are unique yet we share much that constitutes life, and the emotions which define us as human beings.

Life is what happens while you are busy making other plans.

—John Lennon

Once, on a dating site, I encountered a long-haul pilot and I began to think how difficult their privileged, extremely unusual lives must be when beginning a day in one country, on one continent and ending in another, far removed, within a different time zone.

Having always considered it an exciting, somewhat glamorous choice of career, I came to realise that with that also came the possibility of loneliness, of huge challenges in maintaining close relationships when forever on the move and the huge stress to be bourne as a result of continuously disturbed circadian rhythms. May we offer all the world's pilots a smile when next we pass them in an airport, for the service they provide to us.

A Pilot's Life

Tell me what you think of in that head of yours all day
When up above the clouds so high, where you alone can say
How wonderful this life I have, how spectacular the view
Just captain and co-pilot, the others they are few

Tell me what you think of all alone in bed at night
Do you wonder where today you are, do you wake up in a fright
Does your mind spin with the wonder, is it hard to comprehend
How far you've travelled since morning, at time of journey's end

Tell me what you think of when your alarm goes off at four
When the rest of us turn over and sleep a little more
Is excitement of the day to come still in your heart, still strong
Despite the times you've climbed the steps, to the place where you belong

Tell me does your heart race as your hand the lever finds
Thrusting forward, oblivious, of the passengers behind
Is your breath a little faster as you fly down through the cloud
To land that big bird safely on the latest foreign ground

Tell me as you globetrot, do you long for home at all
A love to share the sights with and in bed with which to fall
Someone to cook you breakfast, to hold your hand at night
Someone to tell your dreams to, after the morning's flight

Or does the world you live in bring you heavenly delight
Every journey, every air mile, every time that you alight
Do you yearn to go again, every hour, every minute
To that cockpit in the sky, where the world is without limit

Written for a colleague, one of five extremely close sisters, one of whom passed away some months earlier and another facing treatment for breast cancer during the Covid pandemic, where contact was limited and FaceTime was the only way of providing support.

A Sister Is

How to describe her loving care
A life lived of which we share
Those childhood days so long ago
Where memories lie only we know

The one who knows me best of all
The one to catch me when I fall
The one who boils my blood with rage
With whom sometimes I won't engage

What's life without this sister mine
Together we step back in time
Yet marching forward on we go
To places neither of us yet know

Children raised, families grown
Care and love forever shown
To all new members arriving here
She loves them all, my sister dear

Over tea and wine no details spared
To that other with whom I'm paired
She's seen it all, witnessed all tales
She's been the wind beneath my sails

In darkest days she's standing by
To hear me when I laugh or cry
She buoys me up, she puts me down
She makes me smile, she makes me frown

She'll give advice at any time
Tell how it is for me and mine
She brings me joy, she brings me tears
She strives to wipe away my fears

She's strong, she's bold, she's brave, she's wise
But only I may criticise
For if you dare bring harm to her
It'll be my wrath which you incur

The ties which bind as strong as steel
My inner thoughts they do reveal
A history shared of joys and woes
That keeps in friends and keeps out foes

A relationship that's like no other
A friend, a sage, a surrogate mother
She knows my flaws, accepts me true
My steadfast sister, I love you

Working in a specialist cancer-treatment hospital is both a privilege and a challenge sometimes. It is often an emotional rollercoaster with overload or burnout always posing a major risk. Like so many of my colleagues, I am passionate about my work and about the patients I am able to support however, cancer is a testing disease that if we could, we would choose to eliminate in a heartbeat, putting each and every one of us, immediately out of a job. This was penned during the coronavrius pandemic of 2020 when times became particularly tough with staff facing not one but two deadly diseases. I never ceased to be amazed at how they continued with compassion and empathy in abundance. This is dedicated to all the NHS everyday heroes!

How Many Times

How many times I've sat beside a patient in a bed
Listening to the fears that swirl within their head
How many times seen tears streaming down a face
When the news that blessed tumour, has galloped on apace

How many times I've heard a patient say they can't go on
How they tried with every fibre
Through treatments soldiered on
How many times I've witnessed

Caring colleagues struggle to cope
When a patient in their care is devoid of all hope
How many able nurses have been brought down to their knees
When bodies failing daily seem to be all that they see

How many cups of tea carers make for someone's wife
When husband's final journey has upended her whole life
How many wine bottles consumed at home each night
For a wealth of strong emotions before the next day yet to fight

How many people taken
Way too young, way too soon
Future chances crudely stolen
Opportunities never to bloom

How many times I've passed a weary surgeon in the hall
And wondered of their angst when in bed at night they crawl
How many times I've glimpsed that dreaded terror in someone's eyes
And the havoc these cells wreak this disease we so despise

So we impatiently await the day we hope will come
When your reach is no more and our job is truly done
How we yearn for the day when we have done our best
And it's *you* dying in bed, it's *you* we lay to rest

No more pain, no more suffering
No more families torn apart

No move loved ones enduring
Patients waiting to depart

How we'll dance upon that gravestone
We'll delight with such glee
Then when asked for whom the bell tolls
We'll say cancer it tolls for thee.

They say 'Dogs have owners, cats have slaves'. In my home, this is certainly true. This poem is dedicated to my stray cat Thomas, who was once a street cat enduring all of life's hardships, and now, is the happiest, laziest cat I have ever known with a mistress who dances to his every tune. May every animal find a safe place to lay their head with their own slave to boot!

Lazy Cat

He won't go out, he lies about, no toil for him to do
No mice to catch,
just chairs to scratch
A modern cat through and through

His fur he tends, I'll give him that, his pelt is one to see
But beyond this preening
It's mere daydreaming
Until it's time for tea

Ferociously he guards the flap
Interlopers to deter
They're bold enough to come on in
Risking tufts of fur

A pin-up cat, with features fine
He's certainly a looker
Appealing eyes and mournful mews
He's learnt that I'm a sucker

He lies upon the landing,
in the middle of the floor
Ensures I must stride over him
Careering towards the door

The indoor life, his chosen path
No need for wind or rain
A comfy chair, a nice warm bed
No hardships ever again

As a keen gardener, I love spring. It marks the endurance of long, cold winter months and for me, is the time when we can breathe, hope and live again following this period of hibernation. The joys of watching a tiny seed grow into a young plant or of a plant which I have not seen for many months, reappear, like an old friend, is immeasurable.

Spring

So spring has sprung
A bell has rung
In all of nature's genes
Watch things unfurl
The leaves uncurl
As everything turns green

Birdsong falls
Such vibrant calls

The time to procreate
When nests are made
For fluffy babes
And frosty airs abate

Winter survived
Our souls revived
Hardships we had to bear
Now light relief is on the way
This best time of the year

When lambs leap up
Their mothers tup
Such joy within their soul
When flowers peek
New warmth they seek
Contained within the soil

Anticipation fills our hearts
The seeds which we can sow
Deep in the ground
And all around
Sit back then watch them grow

The garden centres we'll frequent
For topsoil and new shrubs
Then home again
To borders prep
And shoo away the grubs

Then buds appear
And flowers bloom
So wonderful to see
The welcomeness of spring is rife
Affords us all such glee

Bask deeply in the wealth of it
For depart it surely will
To leave us facing glummer months
And pining for it still

Then settle down to wait once more
For it to come again
To bring for us new life, new hope
Return of sun and rain

Two years ago, I moved to a new town, one where homelessness is prevalent and where people with no home sit regularly at sets of traffic lights seeking money, food and compassion. As a result of the Covid-19 pandemic, local councils began housing homeless people in a variety of buildings, in an attempt to lessen the spread of the virus.

I wondered how it was, in 2020, that it took a deadly virus for us to notice people living amongst us, with problems admittedly, but essentially, just like you and me.

Beggar Me

Do you see me on the pavement
As you pass me in the street
Do you wish I wasn't there
As you look down at your feet

Do you see I'm someone's daughter
Once a lover and a friend
Do you see my heart was broken
And will likely never mend

Do you see the can of lager
Which I drink to dull the pain

In your home do you wonder
When I'll see a bed again

Do you see humiliation
On my face and in my eyes
See a stranger's condescension
Or that look of sheer despise

Do you know how cold my feet get
On a frosty winter's morn
See the dullness of my hair
Or my clothing thin and worn

Can you comprehend my fear
Every night as I lay down
Could my life have been different
Imagine if I were renowned

Will you stop and give a moment
From your busy scheduled day
Tear your eyes from your phone
Or simply look the other way

My father is one of the most talented people I know. There is little he can't turn his hand to, in practical terms. In this, his eighty-third-year, it is only now that I myself, having reached a half century, realise the full extent of his talents. During my childhood, he could always be found fixing, making or building something and if he did not know how to do something, he would learn. This 'can do' attitude to life has served him well and has trickled down in varying guises to both his daughters. On behalf of my sister and I, Dad, we salute you. This poem is dedicated to all good fathers everywhere.

Ask My Dad

If you've something in need of repair
And fix it yourself you don't dare
Then my dad's the man
For fix it he can
And he'll do it with consummate flair

He's a shed that's as big as a house
And is probably home to a mouse
If you're needing a dowel
A drill or a trowel
Or a tool which can rid you of louse

Then pop round for he'll have the right tool
Choice enough for a tradesman to drool
Tile cutter or drill
Window box for your sill
Sewing machine in need of a spool

Be it plumbing or electric machinery
A new plant to add to your greenery
He can make one anew
Show you plants that he grew
Build a bench so to view lovely scenery

So don't bin it before dad has looked
And checked to see if it's ****ed
For test it he will
Utilise many a skill
And rarely your goose will be cooked

DIY has the ultimate fan
For my dad is surely the man
Who will bring things to life
With some toil and some strife
Taking things back to where they began

In need of a roof tile or two
Then he'll make you a lot or a few
Fit your tap or your shower
Will not charge by the hour
Even prepare you a drop of home brew

So leave it to Johnny you'll see
How rapidly fixed things can be
With a scratch of his head
He will put it to bed
Any task completed with glee

At the end of June during the 2020 coronavirus pandemic, single people were finally permitted to meet with a person from another household, forming 'a social bubble'. My friend drove the 130 miles from his home to mine in order to stay with me for a few days and we were incredibly fortunate to have two record-breaking 30 degree heat days in which to enjoy the delights of various parks. Several weeks earlier I had happened upon the most beautiful park which I wanted to share with him. Like me, he is an avid 'people watcher' and over the years we have gained much pleasure from imagining the stories behind the people we have observed. Unbeknownst to both of us, this particular park, turned out to be one of the most vibrant parks I have ever had the privilege of visiting and provided a host of characters to make us smile and laugh. From its sunken garden to the wide promenade and the hundreds of mature, elegant trees which fill the park, the wonders of such marvellous outdoor spaces which are free and available to all, amazes me every time I enter.

This is a tribute to all the world's parks and those who planted the saplings which we enjoy today. Parks provide solace, a place to be, think, meet, run and play, for children and adults alike. The world would be a much poorer place without parks.

Park Bench

Here we sit with observing eyes
Watching, waiting for things to spy
A voyeur's pleasure in open view
People busy with things to do

Little girl on her pink bike
Racing round a real delight
With her dolly sat behind
Senses focused, all aligned

Little boys chase one another
Under watchful eye of a grandmother

Hoping adventure here to make
In the shrubbery with twig as rake

Young mums meeting
On wooden seating
Tiny fingers picking gravel
Sense of play to unravel

Children rolling down the hill
Childhood dreams to fulfil
Young lovers snapping photos
Before a fountain, beside the primrose

Man alone reading Dickens
Hard going but to it he's sticking
As the dusk begins to fall
Returning home a wish to stall

Muslim men sat in a circle
Playing cards universal
Feel the grass beneath their feet
Relief at last that they can meet

Young dudes with their homies
Stand together but not too closely
Donning footwear with a tick
Every one looking slick

Married couple sat apart
Perhaps with longings to impart

Cooing gently, laughing low
Planning places where to go

Middle-aged men wearing masks
Keeping fit, completing tasks
Cautious now of what is here
Still a virus which to fear

Ladies walking side by side
A certain age, a sense of pride
Maybe friends or even sisters
Dare to glance at someone's mister

Three young beefcakes seek a girl
Hormones churning in a whirl
One un-shirted proud and fine
Astride the wall in a line

Elderly man sat intent
Thoughts of sins to repent
Mouthing words from The Quran
Trying to be a better man

All life is here, better than TV
Just sit and watch, so much to see
So take some time, frequent a park
All human behaviour, amazing and stark

Having reached my half century, I realise that the old adage, youth is wasted on the young, is true. I wish I had known what I now know, when I was aged 20.

Notes on Ageing

Try as you might
That process you'll fight
The winner you never can be
For 'tis time in control
Her feet they will stroll
All over your face wait and see

Your cheeks they will sag
Beneath each eye a bag
Tram lines run from north to south
Cheeks no longer plump
The Botox you'll pump
To combat that downturned mouth

Your hair it will thin
Daily strands in the bin

That hair dye always to hand
Your makeup inspired
Bucket load now required
Like mixing cement with sand

On the pounds they will go
New love handles to show
Bigger knickers you'll now need to buy
Next size up waiting there
Have that cake if you dare
But remember those scales they don't lie

Your bladder will seep
And will cause you to weep
If a toilet nearby you can't find
Menopause comes along
To sing you her song
Mother Nature being truly unkind

Middle age such a drag
You can no longer brag
Those good looks and fine body no more
Distant memory they are
Only viewed from afar
For time has shown them the door

Still do not despair
All in life is not fair
Those young uns will have their come uppence
For there's wisdom with age

Be the ultimate sage
For my young self I wouldn't give tuppence

Section Two – Love

There is only one happiness in this life, to love and be loved.
—George Sand

Romantic love and particularly the laws of attraction, have long fascinated me, therefore it is unsurprising that it is the focus of many of my poems. Running the gauntlet that is falling in love, provide us with unforgettable experiences and memories that we may treasure or seek to forget, it is a game of Russian Roulette, the outcome seemingly precariously dependent upon the throw of the dice and the whim of Lady Luck.

Go Online

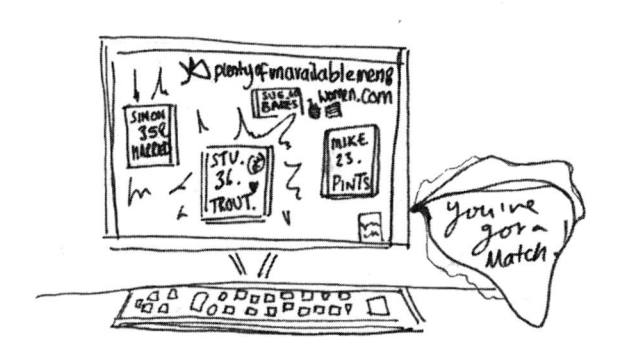

Need a date, a special match
Looking for that perfect catch
Online dating, that's the place for you to be
Have a browse, take your pick
It's so easy, swipe or click
There's a plethora of faces there to see

Now there's Tinder or there's Match
And of course Plenty of Fish
What's the difference, who can say which one's for you
Pay your money, make your choice
Pen a profile, find your voice
Off you go, start to mingle, dates will ensue

Lots of ladies there a-pouting
Laws of physics they'll be flouting
Need an airbrush, paint it out for goodness sake
Dresses donned, legs bared
Filters on, cleavage dared
Heaven forefend someone should say that you're a fake!

Men on pushbikes, scaling mountains
Sporting guns, catching trout
Action men in all their glory everywhere
In the gym, down the pub
Downing pints, eating grub
Ladies please ensure you are 'Buyer Beware'

So you've chatted and you've flirted
Around the baggage you have skirted
And you're off to meet that Mr or Miss Right
Will she stun you, leave you breathless
Will he whisk you off your feet
Or simply leave you in an awful state of fright

Dedicated to all those online daters who got to know each other a whole lot better via WhatsApp and Zoom during lockdown. May the first meeting be everything you hoped it to be.

Chance

Can you hear my thoughts when I think of you
Do you sense my soul from afar
Is there ever a moment's doubt
When you wonder, how bizarre

That the universe should pair us
In the blinking of an eye
When atoms merge together
Hearts and minds unified

Is it chance or fated destiny
In which you place belief
Will our feelings betray us
Will that meeting bring relief

When our eyes behold each other
Will we know deep down within
'Tis the moment much awaited
When a future can begin

So did Cupid play a part
In this fairy tale so sweet

Or is it simply chance occurrence
That allows us now to meet

Do I need to know the answer
Will I submit to higher powers
I care little for the theory
Just so long as true love flowers

It has long been documented that being in love may be akin to a form of madness, where lovers unable to think coherently, will go to extraordinary lengths for the one with whom they are infatuated. This is my tribute to all lovers but in particular, middle-aged ones who face particular challenges of their own.

I Would...

I would follow you
To Timbuktu, Oslo or Japan
Sail around the world in a small canoe
Because you are my man

I would leave my job if you asked me to
Up sticks and simply move
To demonstrate my love for you
In whatever ways you choose

I'd happily walk upon
Hot coals or over liquid fire

For the prospect of life without you
Quite simply would be dire

I would wrestle Bengal Tigers
Swim across an ocean wide
Risk shark-infested waters
Were you on the other side

I would scale the biggest mountain
To stand upon the top
So the world would know my love is real
And which nothing that could stop

I would lay down on a bed of nails
Trek deep into the jungle
Cross the desert through ferocious heat
Before you which to stumble

I would hold my breath until I died
Relinquish all my cash
Just to see that you are smiling
Endure the whippings of a lash

I would live among Amazonian tribes
Be sent up into space
Against the greatest living athletes
Run a hundred metre race

I would dance upon the biggest stage
Even though I've two left feet
I would walk the darkest, meanest streets

With no fear of who I'd meet
I would face the strongest Iron Man
I would learn to fly a plane
I would wait until eternity
Just to see your face again

So now you know just what I'd do
It's clear for all to see
But just for now, sit down my love
Let's have a cup of tea

For I hope you know I love you
That it's plain and in no doubt
Let my words do all the talking
Do I really need go out?

I have often wondered whether is it possible to pinpoint the actual moment when we fall in love, how we transition from a person being a complete stranger to the person our whole world revolves around, the one we are unable to do without. It is a well-trodden path and yet seemingly one which many of us, despite having walked it previously, find difficult to navigate again.
Dedicated to those for whom love springs eternal.

Home For the Heart

A walk alone on a sandy beach
Another's fingers in easy reach
Seated in union on a park bench
The idea of parting a major wrench
Observing strangers through secret eyes
Thoughts in sync with no surprise
To foreign lands we can explore
Leaving us only wanting more
Yet return we shall to that safe home
That inner sanctum where hearts are known
A world enclosed, a sheltered retreat
Where bodies, souls and minds can meet
A place apart for you and I
With dreams realised, satisfaction high
A home for two where love is made
And plans are mooted or conveyed
Where morning breaks and evening calls
The world in limbo where time is stalled
A place of joy where laughter sounds
Where love is king and peace abounds
Solitude disarmed to fade away
And come again some other day
Another's talents duly revered

Achievements rewarded enthusiastically cheered
The place where fears and woes are banished
Doubts swept aside, so easily vanquished
A soul has searched and now has found
Someone to share a life profound
Possibilities abound day after day
So many words for us to say
Memories made, dreams fulfilled
Which serendipity has willed
One of a pair, one half a whole
The missing piece, a mate for soul
So let's begin a lifetime's joy
One single girl, one single boy
Along the road to pastures new
Where we can turn and see where love grew

The laws of attraction are complex and not always easy to fathom. Sitting with a friend, he will often query what it is that one person sees in another. How on earth can I answer? Attraction is personal, what each of us notice about a person, others may fail to see completely. But for many of us, attraction begins with the physical being, a person's hair, their eyes, their body, their gait, their height, may all be contributing factors. Yet attraction begs the question, do we see those we love differently or love those because of what we see? In reality, it probably matters little as our hearts and minds seem to decide our fates for us. Sometimes we are beholden to our desires, often unable to see flaws in others simply because we are consumed by our attraction to a person. Attraction is deliciously compelling and we are often powerless in the face of it. This is my tribute to the men of the world and to give thanks for the beauty and pheromones they possess!

Woman's Joy

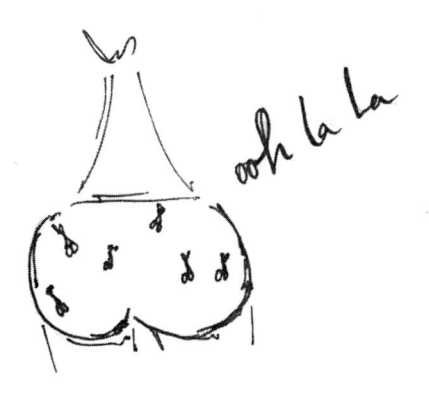

Kiss me slowly, kiss me quick
This joyful habit I cannot kick
I like it long, I like it slow
Always best with one I know

With lips on mine, my passion stirs
Like a cat, my engine purrs
My heart beats fast, my breath will quicken
So please don't leave me feeling stricken

Just tantalise or even tease me
Let those strong arms of yours appease me
Those manly hands do not withhold
A woman likes a man who's bold

Those raunchy words I long to hear
Breathlessly whispered in my ear
Those shoulders wide, that shapely chest
Pressed tightly to my heaving breast

Those muscular arms and long-limbed legs
Leave me feeling inclined to beg
So with me share your precious time
And put your loving hand in mine

Come turn me on, inflame my being
There's little chance that I'll be fleeing
When eyes are closed and you proceed
Excitement surges through veins indeed

Undo that zip, take down these straps
Around your waist let these legs wrap
Let us be naughty, no need for nice
It's time to add some bedroom spice

That pleasing waist, that damn fine chest
For me it is the absolute best
Gentle fingers along my spine
Around my body those arms entwine

When smell of aftershave is strong
It soundly strikes my feminine gong
With biceps firm I yearn to stroke
Waves of longing they do evoke

Taught firm calves I can't resist
From squeezing hard, I can't desist
Toned buttock cheeks are quite the sight
Like lovely cherries I'd like to bite

That jet-black hair upon your head
I want to take you straight to bed
With beautiful hands and forearms too
Is it any wonder I want you

All Things Sweet

Give me a look
At that white sugar cane
For my life without it
Would not be the same
All those sugary treats
Putting holes in my teeth
With only my dentist
Knowing what lies beneath

From biscuits with tea
Or a slice of good cake
That saccharine crack
I cannot forsake
I am hooked that's for certain
I have tried to withdraw
But I manage three days
Then I run to the store
To buy me some chocolate
Some sweeties or cake
Not a thought for my waistline
Need to lessen this ache

Don't need drugs, don't need spirits
Forget wine, keep your beer
It's the lack of a biscuit
That invokes the most fear
So permit me a moment
Allow me a fix
Do not judge by my weakness
All I need's Pick 'n' Mix
Keep your salty, your savoury
Sweet is all I require
'Tis the thing that I live for
My burning desire
Mr Tate Mr Lyle
It is you whom I blame
With your foresight to harvest
That damn sugar cane
If there's ever a time
This addiction I beat
Then life won't be worth living
For there'll be nothing sweet

I have the misfortunate of having inherited a 'sweet tooth' from my maternal grandmother. I readily admit my addiction, and live in hope, that one day, I will look back and be able to say, I no longer covet 'The White Stuff'.

You

To me you are a summer breeze
That follows a winter's night
A mirage in a desert land
Appeared before my sight

The sound of birdsong
Across the morn
The daily breaking of the dawn
The ocean's waves
Amidst the storm
All my passion you ignite

The music made by your own voice
Lands gently on my ear
A sound I yearn for always
To be forever near

Your words are like the softest kiss
That cause my soul to yield in bliss
May they be something I never miss
In my heart, forever dear

I wonder of my life before
The day you reached my romantic shore
Your soul has travelled far to reach
My boundary walls it sought to breach
A lesson you knew how to teach
A message to my very core
To me you are the air I need
To breathe another day
To change, to grow, to love, to say
All the things that must be said
No feelings now of fear or dread
From mine own heart to your own head
Let this be the only way

When we are fortunate enough to find our soulmate, there is always a beginning, a time when we were not sure, a getting to know each other time, a time filled with possibility and hope, a time when we yearn to know everything inside that person's head. We can of course never actually realise the entire contents of a partner's head, yet the desire to do so, particularly in those early weeks and months, is strong. We almost wish away that precious learning time, wanting to skip ahead, to the point where we are comfortable in our learned knowledge, akin to gaining the skills to master a new piece of equipment, without having to read the manual. 'Look Inside' is my attempt, in poetry terms at least, to focus on these precious moments, and to provide my Mr Right, and perhaps that of many women, with the requisite manual.

Look Inside

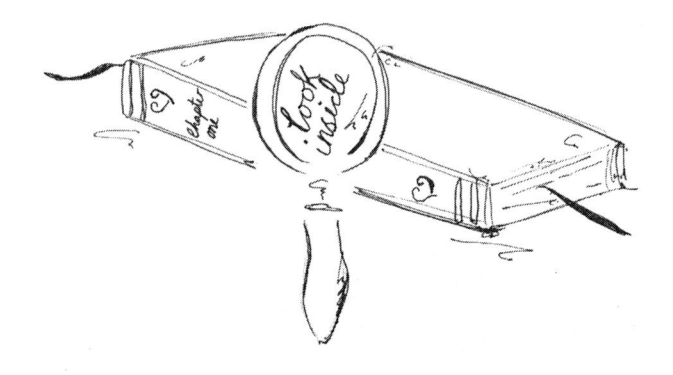

If you'd like to get to know me
Take some time spare a thought
Do not bring expensive perfume
For this woman can't be bought

What you'll need's a little patience
Lots of love along the way
Show respect and understanding
Listen to all she has to say

Treat her gently like a pony
Do not scare her or she'll flee
Be tenacious don't give up

You'll be where she longs to be
Give her laughter bring her joy
Every time when you've a chance
Shore her up if she needs it
Do not look at her askance

Bring her kisses soft and tender
Fuel the passion in her heart
Let her go the way she wants to
You'll be off to a good start

Let her know how much you need her
Say the words she needs to hear
When you have something worth saying
Whisper softly in her ear

Show reliance and forgiveness
Be the best that you can be
If you want her to love you
Be the only man she'll see

Lay your soul down at her altar
Your emotions do not hide
Be ever truthful with your words
And her heart will open wide

So here's the message you should follow
It's so simple once you know
Gain her trust, her love, her essence
And her everything she'll show

How Strange Love Is

Sneakily, creepily, surprises us
Worries, hurries, teases us
Delights, frights, deceives us
Enchants, decants, then dies with us

The Things You Do

You make me smile
You make me feel
You make me want to love again
You make me think
Reveal my soul
Be better than I've ever been

You make me long to hear your voice
You make me want to touch your face
To hear your fears to soothe your pain
You make me laugh
You build me up
So I can breathe and live again

You make me strong
You make me weak
You fill my heart with hope and light
Say things I sometimes dare not speak
You make me look
You make me wait
For that future burning bright

You see my soul
You know my heart
A wonder I could not foretell
You stoke my fire
With icy cool
That makes me gasp as passions swell
You make me bold
You make me shy
Lay me bare unfurl my being
You stretch my mind
My thoughts unleash
With your eyes only truly seeing

You turn me on
You make me want
To run my fingers through your hair
Your lips on mine
My skin on yours
My very own to treat with care

Of all the many things you do
Of all the feelings which are true
The wonder of your inner soul
The power over me you hold
'Tis truly wondrous to behold
The beautiful essence that is you

If

If I were a butterfly and you were the breeze
Together we'd drift in relative ease
Up in the mountains and over the streams
Together forever in search of our dreams

If I were a pebble and you were the sea
Always and forever together we'd be
Waves gently lapping upon the shore
Hard to imagine what there was before

Think Of Me

Think of me
Within your mind
Memories forever
There confined

Think of me
When first you wake
In hazy tones
Before daybreak

Think of me
When feeling blue
Reliving how
Those feelings grew

Think of me
So far away
When wanting home
Needing to stay

Think of me
Amidst your fear

When all alone
Wish I was near

Think of me
When in bed you lie
See me clear
In your mind's eye

Think of me
In your hopes and dreams
When life is not
All that it seems

And if this love
Of ours should break
Then think of me
For old time's sake

Section Three – Hope

Hope is being able to see that there is light despite all of the darkness.

—Desmond Tutu

There is little doubt, we are charting difficult waters. The Covid pandemic tested humanity across the world, wreaking havoc amidst us, changing our lives as we could not have imagined. We continue to live with the consequences. We also continue to face the challenge that is global warming, the greatest ever faced by mankind. Alongside this, parts of the world have seen major shifts in the political landscape, creating uncertainty and division, and with war once again on the continent of Europe, millions of lives have been thrust into extraordinary hardship.

Despite these challenges, we have seen a resurgence of hope, a coming together, an understanding of our connectedness to one another, a recognition of the requirements of good mental health, and a far greater understanding of the need to protect and care for the natural world.

In a sick society, hope is the very best medicine. We must continue to hope that together, we are capable of great things, and it is this hope which will provide the belief and the necessary momentum to propel us to the better times which lie ahead.

In 2018, a 15-year-old Greta Thunberg galvanised the world's children to leave their school desks and make their voices known to political leaders in a bold attempt to power the issue of climate change up to the top of the political agenda. This is a tribute to her.

The Wonder of Youth

To Greta we are grateful, for focusing our mind
To the plight of the environment, of which we have been blind
Around the world in 80 days, she travels on and on
Her message shouted loud and clear, to climate change, Be Gone!

We can't afford to wait, she says, of this we can be sure
Yet all the world's great leaders, prevaricate once more
Her mission is straightforward, determination in abundance
No use in children in their schools, they soon shall be redundant.

Such wisdom in so young a mind, she's history in the making
Her task not easy, yet shoulders broad, for the biggest undertaking
She stands for good, unites us all, humanity together
Remember Greta for all time, she made the world much better

I have loved the natural world for as long as I can remember, from the hedgehog or songbirds who frequent our gardens to the amazing, big cats and the habitats in which they are king, from Peru to Afghanistan. Hearing David Attenborough narrate the many wildlife documentaries which have punctuated both my childhood and adult life, instilled a yearning to learn more and to protect the millions of species we are privileged enough to share this Earth with. I believe we have a duty of care towards all life on this amazing planet, to protect it and appreciate it for all the wondrous joys it provides us. This is my tribute to all our fellow species, large and small.

Did You Ever

Did you ever stop to wonder why the grass is always green
Why a lesser-spotted woodpecker prefers to go unseen
Did it ever cross your mind that the sea's not really blue
But that the light's refraction has you believing that it's true

Did you gaze upon the stars and wonder how many that there are
Or how very small our Earth is when viewed from afar
Have you sat and pondered why it is that penguins have short legs
Or how tiny are their steps and the questions which that begs

Is there any harm in asking why that leopard has those spots
Or how the blood within her body separates or clots
Does the magic of the universe give you cause to stop and think
Do you hunger to know, do you thirst for that drink

Are there questions of which science has no answer to provide
Can we look with eyes anew, place our knowledge to one side
Is it merely human nature to want to know the reasons why
At every given opportunity, invariably we pry

Of the millions of wonders which are out there to behold
Every miniscule particle with a story to be told
Will we ever fully gain all the answers that we seek
Can we act in humble deference, are we able to become meek

Do we see with our eyes open, have we ever truly known
How the world came into being, all the wonders it has shown
Do the leaves from that old oak tree make you glad that trees are there
Standing tall, proud and graceful, filtering our air
Do we need to learn to care for every being that is here
Can we live with ourselves, have our hearts without fear
Do we need to stop a moment and appreciate it all
Or will our arrogance lead us to the saddest downfall

Do you ever really think just how little that we know
How our choosing not to learn, lessens how we grow
Does Mother Nature hold the answer, does she care for us to stay
Or simply yearn for the time when we have had our day

In January 2017, Donald Trump was inaugurated as president of the United States.

On May 25th 2020, the brutal death of George Floyd at the hands of a US police officer, rocked the land of the free and sent ripples across the world.

This is a tribute to all those who stand up against injustice and inhumanity, wherever it rears its ugly head.

God Bless America

Leader of the free world
The man to whom we look
Though seemingly it's obvious
He doesn't give a ****

A man to whom the world's a stage
A circus in which to play
A plethora of platforms
Where one can have a say

A mouthpiece to the nation
That good old USA
With guns and war and hatred
The order of the day

One man, one view, one vision
A population stable
Where any dream is realised
If only one is able

No matter if you're rich or poor
For little do we care
It's profit margins that we seek
It's those we want to share

Yet if your face is coloured brown
Or black as coal can be
If Spanish is your mother tongue
Then frankly heaven help thee
He'll build a wall to keep you out
Incite others against you
It's unity in coloured tribes
Do as I say not as I do

Brutality in Minneapolis
America is burning
Yet he's still in The White House
And the world just keeps on turning

So God send America
All the help that she can get

For Trump seeks re-election
And his term's not over yet

No lessons learned from history
No wisdom which to share
Going backwards and not forwards
How is any of it fair

Democracy they asked for
Democracy they got
So be grateful all Americans
And beware his parting shot
For he longs to leave a legacy
Worst or best, he does not care
All the words remain on Twitter
So the whole world can despair

2020 will be a year that will live long in the memories of millions, for one reason, the Covid-19 global pandemic. This is a tribute to the many who tragically lost their lives, may they rest in peace and their souls live on in those of us who remain.

Dreaded Virus

It's Coronavirus madness, it's got us in a panic,
Shoppers flee to Sainsbury's, everyone is manic,
No toilet roll, no pasta, no hand wash to be had,
No coffee cake with friends for months, it's making me quite sad.

I turn on the TV, I watch the news with dread,
Men in plastic suits and boots, I'd rather not know instead,
In Italy, in China, Dubai and Leningrad,
We're all in it together, your friend, your neighbour, your dad.

Self isolate's the message, stay home from work, and play,
Wash those hands thoroughly, at least 20 times a day.
Sing to 'Happy Birthday', hold those hands beneath the tap,
Avoid people like the plague, arms around, do not wrap.

Leave my parcels at the door, my groceries on the step,
To visitors who ring my bell, inside I will not let.
It's me, myself, the radio, no frivolous chitty chat,
I've no one left to talk to, except the blasted cat.

I need to muster spirit, a Kitchener-esque approach,
To dig deep in the freezer, finally cook that poxy roach.
So I'll hunker down for now, write a letter, dust my shelves,
And hope that by year end we can all become ourselves.